QUITE HAPPY

POEMS

LC WILLIAMS

First Print Edition

Produced and Distributed By:

Library Partners Press
ZSR Library
Wake Forest University
1834 Wake Forest Road
Winston-Salem, North Carolina 27106

www.librarypartnerspress.org

ABOUT THE POEMS

"But what one does realize is that, when you try to stand up and look the world in the face like you had a right to be here, when you do that, without knowing that this is the result of it, you have attacked the entire power structure of the western world."
– James Baldwin

"The most common way people give up their power is by thinking they don't have any."
– Alice Walker

"Sometimes I don't want to be a soldier. Sometimes I just wanna be a man."
– Mos Def

To be black and happy in America is a fundamental paradox and a constant struggle. I am charged with loving this country unconditionally, even when I feel it doesn't love me.

Originally, these poems were titled *Quite Happy: Poems on Black Life.* Although accurate, that title did not capture what I hope is the universality of the sentiments contained in the chapbook. For example, I think many women, regardless of color/race/identity, struggle with a perceived perpetual availability. Likewise, I think many Southerners understand that sweet tea is not a vice, but a summertime staple. So, while these poems reflect my thoughts on my black life – which is distinctly, although not "tragically" black – I hope they connect with all readers.

Marshall McLuhan is quoted as saying "publication is a self–invasion of privacy." He also said that "the future of the book is the blurb." *Quite Happy* is both. The poems contained here are abbreviated versions of secret and difficult conversations. Truth is often painful. Yet, I choose to keep grasping for it…to make sense of the utter senseless. And, frankly, when I am justifiably angry – at the historical maltreatment and the current disregard of blackness – I harbor those thoughts long enough to taste and spit them out. Regardless of the situation, my natural tendency is toward happiness…to find, as Black Star rapped, "beauty in the hideous."

ABOUT THE COVER

The cover of this book features a photo of my great-grandmother, Daisy M. Foster. I assume it was taken in the 1940s, but I have no evidence to support this. I have little memory of her; she died when I was very young. This photo is a favorite, though, because I imagine that something made her mad but she took the picture anyway.

QUITE HAPPY

POEMS

LC WILLIAMS

For us. In spite of it all.

*"...because they never understand
Black love is Black wealth and they'll
probably talk about my hard childhood
and never understand that
all the while I was quite happy."*

From Nikki Giovanni, "Nikki-Rosa"
from Black Feeling, Black Talk, Black
Judgment. Copyright © 1968, 1970 by
Nikki Giovanni.

TABLE OF CONTENTS

1.   For Snoop, p. 5

2.   Geopathology, p. 7

3.   Abandoned Aprons, p. 9

4.   Meanwhile, in America..., p.11

5.   Ain't There, p.13

6.   For DuBois, p. 15

7.   Weaving, p. 17

8.   Watching You Dance, p. 19

9.   Resignation, p. 21

10.   Ain't Sweet, p. 23

11.   diallo*, p. 25

12.   Sister Speak, p. 29

13. Rummaging, p. 31

14. Chamber Play, p. 35

15. The If/Then Promise
(Hypothetical Revolt), p. 37

16. Good Face, p. 41

17. For Gil Scott, p. 43

18. The Mother Aborted*, p. 45

*"Diallo" and "The Mother Aborted"
originally appeared in the 2001 edition
of **Can-I-Poet-With-You?**.*

FOR SNOOP

In the space between time
and memories you sat unscathed
but scarred sweetly street.
Stoic grace, gender bent.

Game lessons hidden
under hoods, in braid creases.
Clear bags and weighted dice and
you,
in the alley's womb

Defiant, you refused to be killed.
No struggle. No plea.
Power in your palm,
smooth hand swept your
silhouette.

You spoke of loyalties
(ever the consummate soldier)
while clock hands shook
and questions spilled.

A moment's disgust.
A separation of brothers.
Cain's sister
handsomely done.

Mirror shards suspended in air
as your prettiness appears and
retreats
before the farewell:

"How my head look, Mike?"
"You look good, girl."

"GEOPATHOLOGY: A PROBLEM WITH PLACE."
(Term by Una Chaudhuri)

No peace settling here.
This is no home.

I am mother and wife.
These identities
heavy on me like
baby weight and responsibility.

Back there I was *so* good.
That girl in the nineties
driving the indigo convertible.
"She is going places," they all
said.
Everywhere was wide open.

I am mother and wife:
inhabiting this new space.
Beckoned and called.
Now they say, "she is
dependable."
Available.

I am where the new ones
need me: on my knees
giving salve and solace.
So they can be comfortable.
Here.

ABANDONED APRONS

*In the late 1800s a mayor decreed
that black women would only be
allowed in the streets if they were
wearing an apron.*

Crack of dawn
Memories of my grandmother

     Straightening up.
     Coffee brewing.

     She bathed last night.

     Housecoat and slippers on.
     Warm, wet washcloth wiped
     away signs of sleep.

"Grits will stick to your
ribs."

On the side of the bed, my legs
find their first footing.
I try to remember what clothes
are clean for me, my daughter.

Quick showers.
Mismatched socks.

I put her oatmeal in the
microwave. Add butter, brown
sugar.

We put on suits and skirts
and set out for another day.
Practiced platitudes and folios in
hand.

MEANWHILE, IN AMERICA...

1% perks
Talking heads gawk
The system works
And Zimmerman walks

Kimye births
We Twitter-stalk
The system works
And Zimmerman walks

While Miley twerks
And Jay Z talks
The system works
And Zimmerman walks

Our sad, short worth
Outlined in chalk
While a system that works
Lets Zimmerman walk.

AIN'T THERE

I have journeyed
through sizes 6 and up
to land in the world of
14s and 16s.
Although I want to embrace all
this
I am not there yet.
My jiggly tummy is not a source
of pride at having borne three
children.
It is a gelatinous reminder of
cheesecakes past and mason jars
full of sweet tea.
My figure resembles Saartjie
Baartman.
Although I embrace my
steatopygia,

I wouldn't mind carrying just a
little less ass.
My thighs are strong in their
thickness and girth - I do delight
in wrapping them around his
waist...
But it will be nice when they are a
bit more toned.
Then I might actually wear shorts
again.
I look back on that teenaged girl
with arms akin to Michelle
Obama and a waist so lean...
I know that I have
metamorphosed into
this grown woman body.
But I have a lot
more growing to do
before I fully accept
who my body says I am.

FOR DUBOIS

This split self
musing what it ought be
in a world where twoness is
as common as poverty.

WEAVING

Yes, blankets come to mind but
moreso is the thought of you,
little one,
woven together with tiny threads
of your father and me.
Little slivers of my skin and his
black brown eyes,
his sweet dimples, my thick,
black curls.

You are our tapestry, one we
didn't even know we were
creating, purely organic - out of a
completeness that is eternal.

You babble and push and crawl
and toddle
and it amazes me that we were
conduits.
Our creativity blushes in the face
of you, little one,
with your silly little eight-toothed
laugh.

And we are inextricable, under
and over and round and through,
we're part of the same line, the
same thread needled us.

As we grow and unravel, you will
be wrapping pieces of your father
and I in your palm.
You will cuddle the softness that
we've become and, if we are still
lucky,
you will take our fraying ends
and make something beautiful.

WATCHING YOU DANCE

Watching you dance
is like watching birds tease
each other.
Limb over limb
they play, call, tempt.
You are having fun in your world.
No knowledge of my eye on you
as you dance and dance and
dance...
Clapping your tiny little hands
three hours past midnight.
You dance while you think we're
all asleep.

In your own happy world,
you are king and artist,
master and joy.
Full footsteps, flailing arms –
My little boy
dancing.

RESIGNATION

There is a certain joy
in realizing that a
sigh
is the heaviest
exhale -
the necessary
pushing out
destined
to begin
again.

AIN'T SWEET

Truths are less bitter
than the lies
but they surely ain't sweet.
Like knowing
what's real before someone
shames you into
understanding.
This shit here ain't sweet.
We ain't better.
Things ain't better.
We ain't making progress.
We are still "a servile" bunch of
baboons
"childlike in imagination" said the
man from
Harvard, keeper of knowledge He.
They. Them.

Not us. Because shit ain't sweet.
And the man made it so plain
that I had to check myself.
We have the only person who
might give a damn in place to
actually
try to give a damn
and we ask him for nothing
because he's there. And his being
there is enough for us.
And that's important. But when
he's gone
in our lifetime,
in our children's lifetime
won't be nothing left.

DIALLO

They did what they were trained
to do.
They did what they were trained
to do.
Shit, it might as well be the
1940s when people tried to
convict white supremacists for
lynching/castrating black males.
Not guilty, not guilty, not guilty,
not guilty.
They did what they were trained
to do.
They did what they were trained
to do.
What they were trained to do was
kill.
They killed.

That is what they were trained to
do.
They killed him in cold blood in
front of his home.
They took his life, killed his hope,
because they were trained to kill.
They did what they were trained
to do.
They were trained to kill.
Kill.
Kill. Kill. Kill.
They killed him.
His family cries because their son
doesn't matter.
He is nothing.
His death is a mistake.
Sorry.
What have we done?
I acted on impulse.
Please don't die.
I hope those words riddle the
pleasant thoughts of the men who
killed killed killed killed.
Please don't die.
Please don't die.

But if you die it really doesn't
manner.
Because they only did what they
were trained to do. They were
trained to kill
Kill. Kill. Kill. They did what they
were trained to do. Kill.
They are trained to kill you. Kill
you, kill you. kill you.
We don't matter.

SISTER SPEAK

Sitting in this space with you I
feel
a kinship
a oneness and I know you're
miles away from me
in age
in time. Still
we click. We connect as if Legos.
I am a mother, you are not
but you understand my need to
care
my aching compassion
my desire to raise a strong
daughter
and love my boy
before a world breaks him.

You get that I have never been
told what I can't do
I have been, and you and your
boyfriend, too, have been told
that we could be president
or lawyers and doctors.
We talk about whether this is a
curse or a blessing because we
may aspire to
anything/everything/nothing.

We have good conversation. This
sister speak
nourishes us.

RUMMAGING

We spent Saturday sifting
through your dead things.
Letters, trinkets, boxes inside
boxes, keys and clothes.
I found a picture of you with my
daddy on your lap.
He was 5ish, so you couldn't be
more than 18.
Pretty, but older than you needed
to be.
You should've have been
courting, but you were a mother
of a big boy and had to work that
much harder.
I wonder what your life was like.
Why things seemed so rough for
you.

Why you needed love so much
more than the boy could provide.
Why you'd love men who couldn't
love you.
I have seen traces of that in my
loving.
I hope this mutation seeps away
before my daughter tries love out.

My daddy looks at me from the
picture with my son's eyes and
cheekbones.
You carry the weight and depth of
your heavy life in your neck, your
chest.

We rummaged through your dead
things finding items no one
should hold onto.
He had kept your casket key. A
cold reminder that you lived and
died and were now buried in
Evergreen.

When I miscarried the doctor told
us, in a sterile, medical way, that

we had in fact created a baby that
lived briefly and had died.
I assume she had to tell us that
so we wouldn't conjure some
crazy other idea about the
growing child we'd initially
rejected.
I always remember the doctor
looking as if it didn't really matter
that we were heartbroken.
That she was granting us a mercy
in letting us know that this
journey had begun and ended
abruptly.
Without our consent or control.
"Losing" the baby seemed easier.
Knowing it "died" was another
kick deep in my empty gut.

Going through your dead things
gave me that feeling again.
That empty gut feeling like there
was something missing in a place
you once filled.
This house was where you lived
and ate and hopefully loved. This

is where we watched 227 and
Amen and Golden Girls and
Empty Nest. Where we ate fish on
Fridays and greens on Sundays
after church.
This is where a part of my
childhood lived. And now it's
gone. Has been gone for some
time now but on Saturday
rummaging those feelings came
back.
I wish I'd been alone to fully
absorb you in the space. But, I
have this picture. This image of
you I'd never seen looking so
pretty and polite and motherly at
18...too many years earlier than
you would have liked.
But there you smile nonetheless.

CHAMBER PLAY

He was angry for something...I
can't remember what now.
When he tired of hitting me
he decided to line the children
against the wall in our kitchen.
Their little faces shiny wet, the
whites of their eyes steady, their
hands cold.
The outlines of my babies' heads
trembled on the wall; they were
afraid to look at me.
My reasoning with him, my
attempts to deflect the attention
failed.
I tried to get him to hit me again,
said I'd do anything he wanted.

But he liked to play games when
he was angry.
He stared at me.
The gun's barrel at my tiniest
baby's temple
Pull,
Turn,
Click.
Hours between each motion of
the chamber.
Each of my children only a
chance to him:
a roll of the dice,
a spin of the wheel,
one shot in seven.

THE IF/THEN PROMISE (HYPOTHETICAL REVOLT)

If institutionalized racism murders my child, I can guarantee that:
I will not be poised.
I will not be peaceful.
I will not be rational.
I will not be resilient.
I will not call for peaceful protests.
I will not quote MLK.
I will not accept pity.
I will not praise the intentions of the justice system.
I will not ask people to be nonviolent.

I will not put on a brave face.
I will not seek calm.

I will be angry. And I will enlist
others to join in my anger.

We will burn cars and throw
bottles.
We will break shop windows.
We will scream "Fuck the Po-lice"
until our
throats dry and the veins throb
hard under our
skin.

And if I go it alone
I will dismantle the flawed system
brick by brick
with fiery focus
and a hatred so palpable
love will not be able to force it
out.

I will carry the burden
of these decaying black and
brown bodies
until I join their ranks.

And I will be justified.
Because for me
this has always been and
will be
personal.

GOOD FACE

The man said I had a
good face
which prompted me to think
all other parts of me
were not good.
Then I looked at the man
and understood his compliment:
I had a *good face*.
That was enough.

FOR GIL SCOTT

As your life burned
you stood:
wick in wax.

They called you an addict.

Thinning, you grew worn.
Hands no longer hands.
Awkward beauty.
A dead tree standing as a
hollowed reminder of what the
sun once loved.

You would succumb.
We watched you stagger.
Your pulse the city's beat;
splintered songs in your pocket

saved for a rainy day
or a come up.

Consumed, we did not give you
away.
We nursed you on the bottle we
knew so
intimately.

Even if you died
curled up in a final fix
under the foulness of rotting life,
we savored your sullied beauty.

You were no addict.

Like us
you were caked in soot,
cleaning yourself
the only way you knew how.

THE MOTHER ABORTED

"Push hard, now...
a little while longer,
love"

hands pull life from inside.
child. mother. creation.
birth surges. pivotal points of
pressure and –
the struggle begins.

I remember when I did not know
you,
when thoughts were scrambled
and desire froze.
the ancestors told me you were
always there, though,

they carried you in earthen
pottery,
a mass of coal, woven hair
covered tender flesh,
their crowns balanced as to
steady heaviness,
black papooses strapped on tired
backs,
thin knees creaked and the walk
is longer.

trembling things embrace tense
pain,
cobalt sweat seeks refuge in
crinkled forehead crevices,
muddy brown eyes, once as
polished maple, plead for mercy
knowing it is not deserved,
begging nonetheless...

"almost there,
baby, almost
harder again, once more
once more"

notes soar like the thump of
tribal drums,
bellowing mellow "hummmmms,"
rumbling in throats
parched from constant choking—
stifled spittle settled there after
the screams.

"coming
now, almost here...
push!
look honey,
look..."

night covered her in a cloak of fire
and femininity,
she bled brutal bronze and
you...you journeyed here alone,
leaving her love there,
entering our world with the
thunder of generations in native
tongues.
your voice chanted back to the
ancestors a psalm...
and they praised God for you.

ABOUT THE AUTHOR

Lamaya Covington Williams, aka LC Williams, has received awards for her writing, including the 2001 A.D. Ward medal from Wake Forest University. Her work has appeared in the *Wake Forest University Philomathesian* and *Can-I-Poet-With-You?* series, as well as *The Winston-Salem Journal* and other publications.

She has been guest lecturer at Bennett College, Wake Forest University, and the University of Florida. She teaches humanities at Forsyth Technical Community College.

Made in the USA
Lexington, KY
31 January 2016